THE Best-Ever Kids' KNOCK KNOCK JokeBook

ARCTURUS

ARCTURUS

This edition published in 2015 by Arcturus Publishing Limited
26/27 Bickels Yard, 151–153 Bermondsey Street,
London SE1 3HA

Copyright © Arcturus Holdings Limited

ISBN: 978-1-78404-273-8
CH003744NT
Supplier: 29, Date 0715, Print run 4248

Printed in China

CONTENTS

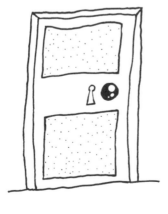

HAIR-RAISING!

Knock, knock...

Who's there?

Ellie.

Ellie who?

Ellie Funt.

Knock, knock...

Who's there?

Tristan.

Tristan who?

Tristan insect to get up
your nose!

Knock, knock...

Who's there?

Zombie.

Zombie who?

Zombies make honey, others
are queens!

Knock, knock...

Who's there?

Hair.

Hair who?

Hair today, gone tomorrow!

Knock, knock...

Who's there?

Eileen Dover.

Eileen Dover who?

Eileen Dover your fence
and broke it!

Knock, knock...

Who's there?

Alien.

Alien who?

Just how many aliens do you know?

Knock, knock...

Who's there?

Phil.

Phil who?

Phil this bag with money,
I'm a robber!

Knock, knock...

Who's there?

The doorbell repairman!

✳

Knock, knock...

Who's there?

Superman.

Superman who?

You know I can't reveal
my secret identity!

✳

Knock, knock...

Who's there?

Albert.

Albert who?

Albert you don't know
who this is!

Knock, knock...

Who's there?

Canoe.

Canoe who?

Canoe come out and play today?

Knock, knock...

Who's there?

Geezer.

Geezer who?

Geezer couple of minutes
and I'll pick the lock.

Knock, knock...

Who's there?

Stan.

Stan who?

Stan back, I'm breaking
the door down!

Knock, knock...

Who's there?

Twitter.

Twitter who?

Have you got an owl in there?

Knock, knock...

Who's there?

Police.

Police who?

Police let me in, it's freezing
out here!

Knock, knock...

Who's there?

Irish stew.

Irish stew who?

Irish stew in the name
of the law!

Knock, knock...

Who's there?

Butter.

Butter who?

Butter bring an umbrella, it looks
like it might rain!

Knock, knock...

Who's there?

Donut.

Donut who?

Donut open until
Christmas!

✸

Knock, knock...

Who's there?

Anka.

Anka who?

Anka the ship!

✸

Knock, knock...

Who's there?

Doris.

Doris who?

Doris jammed, that's why
I had to knock.

Knock, knock...

Who's there?

Granny.

Granny who?

Knock knock.

Who's there?

Granny.

Granny who?

Knock, knock.

Who's there?

Aunt.

Aunt who?

Aunt you glad that Granny's gone?

Knock, knock...

Who's there?

Jacklyn.

Jacklyn who?

Jacklyn Hyde!

Knock, knock...

Who's there?

Carrie.

Carrie who?

Carrie the bags into the house please!

Knock, knock...

Who's there?

Donna.

Donna who?

Donna sit under an apple tree with anyone but me...!

Knock, knock...

Who's there?

A man.

A man who?

A man with a wooden leg.

Tell him to hop it!

Knock, knock...

Who's there?

Ally.

Ally who?

Allygator.

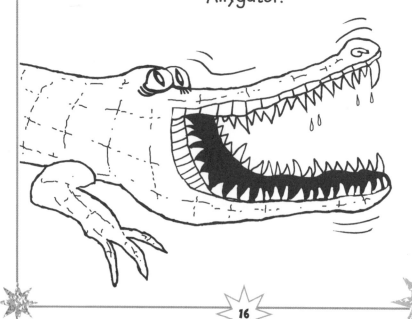

Knock, knock...

Who's there?

Sonia.

Sonia who?

Sonia shoe. I can smell it from here.

Knock, knock...

Who's there?

Howell.

Howell who?

Howell you have your toast?
With marmalade or honey?

Knock, knock...

Who's there?

Munchin.

Munchin who?

Munchin my dinner and
need a drink.

Knock, knock...

Who's there?

Paul.

Paul who?

Paul lady who just fell in a puddle!

Knock, knock...

Who's there?

Cora.

Cora who?

Cora wish I had a front door
like this!

Knock, knock...

Who's there?

Lucy.

Lucy who?

Lucy Lastic. My pants
are falling down!

Knock, knock...

Who's there?

Chimney.

Chimney who?

Chimney cricket! Have you seen Pinocchio?

＊

Knock, knock...

Who's there?

Aida.

Aida who?

Aida whole village 'cos I'm a monster!

＊

Knock, knock...

Who's there?

Arch.

Arch who?

Are you catching a cold?

Knock, knock...

Who's there?

Whoopi.

Whoopi who?

Whoopi cushion!

Knock, knock...

Who's there?

Alec.

Alec who?

Alec my lollipop!

Knock, knock...
Who's there?
Lee King.
Lee King who?
Lee King bucket.

Knock, knock...
Who's there?
Donalette.
Donalette who?
Donalette the bed bugs bite!

Knock, knock...
Who's there?
Hali.
Hali who?
Halitosis – your breath stinks!

Knock, knock...

Who's there?

Aba.

Aba who?

Aba'out turn. Quick march!

✳

Knock, knock...

Who's there?

Aleta.

Aleta who?

Aleta from your teacher!

✳

Knock, knock...

Who's there?

Argo.

Argo who?

Argo to dance class
after school!

Knock, knock...

Who's there?

Alf.

Alf who?

Alf all if you don't catch me!

Knock, knock...

Who's there?

Vera.

Vera who?

Vera long way from home
and need a map!

Knock, knock...

Who's there?

Carter.

Carter who?

Carter stray dog - is it yours?

Knock, knock...

Who's there?

Nana.

Nana who?

Nana your business!

Knock, knock...

Who's there?

Althea.

Althea who?

Althea in court!

✳

Knock, knock...

Who's there?

Army.

Army who?

Army aunts coming for dinner?

✳

Knock, knock...

Who's there?

Baby Owl.

Baby Owl who?

Baby Owl see you later,
baby not!

Knock, knock...

Who's there?

Betty.

Betty who?

Betty earns a lot of money!

Knock, knock...

Who's there?

Tella.

Tella who?

Tella your friends this joke!

*

Knock, knock...

Who's there?

Augusta.

Augusta who?

Augusta wind blew my
hat away!!

Knock, knock...

Who's there?

Benin.

Benin who?

Benin hell. It was awful!

Knock, knock...

Who's there?

Frank.

Frank who?

Frankenstein!

Hi, I'm Frank!

Knock, knock...
Who's there?
Aunt.
Aunt who?
Aunt you glad to see me again!

Knock, knock...
Who's there?
Cliff.
Cliff who?
Cliff hanger!

Knock, knock...
Who's there?
Bertha.
Bertha who?
Berthaday girl!

Knock, knock...

Who's there?

Bacon.

Bacon who?

Bacon a cake for your birthday!

Knock, knock...

Who's there?

Sadie.

Sadie who?

Sadie magic word
and watch me disappear!

Knock, knock...

Who's there?

Ben Hur.

Ben Hur who?

Ben Hur an hour –
let me in!

Knock, knock...

Who's there?

Bee.

Bee who?

Bee a pal and open the door.

Knock, knock...

Who's there?

Bill.

Bill who?

Bill-ding's on fire!

Knock, knock...

Who's there?

Viper.

Viper who?

Viper nose, it keeps running!

Knock, knock...

Who's there?

Avon.

Avon who?

Avon to drink your blood!

Knock, knock...

Who's there?

Dishes.

Dishes who?

Dishes the police! Open up!

✳

Knock, knock...

Who's there?

Cecile.

Cecile who?

Cecile th-the windows. Th-there's
a m-monster out there.

Knock, knock...

Who's there?

Alec.

Alec who?

Alec-tricity. Isn't that a shock?

Knock, knock...

Who's there?

Chopin.

Chopin who?

Chopin in the supermarket.

Knock, knock...

Who's there?

Caesar.

Caesar who?

Caesar jolly good fellow!

✳

Knock, knock...

Who's there?

Betty.

Betty who?

Betty ya don't know who this is!

✳

Knock, knock...

Who's there?

Duck.

Duck who?

**Just duck – they're throwing
things at us!**

Knock, knock...

Who's there?

Carlo.

Carlo who?

Carload of junk!

Knock, knock...

Who's there?

Muffin.

Muffin who?

Muffin the matter with me.
How about you?

Knock, knock...

Who's there?

Spider.

Spider who?

Spider what everyone says,
I like you!

Knock, knock...

Who's there?

Carmen.

Carmen who?

Carmen *like best* is a Ferrari!

✳

Knock, knock...

Who's there?

Kari.

Kari who?

Kari on like this and I'll freeze
to death out here!

Knock, knock...

Who's there?

Cello.

Cello who?

Cello, how are you?

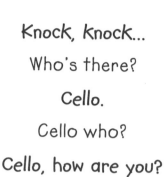

Knock, knock...

Who's there?

Atlas.

Atlas who?

Atlas it's the weekend!

Knock, knock...

Who's there?

Jester.

Jester who?

Jester minute,
I'm trying to find
my keys!

Knock, knock...

Who's there?

Aries.

Aries who?

Aries a reason I'm knocking
at your door!

Knock, knock...

Who's there?

Guthrie.

Guthrie who?

Guthrie blind mice!

Knock, knock...

Who's there?

Congo.

Congo who?

Congo into the woods,
it's dangerous!

Knock, knock...

Who's there?

Tom Sawyer.

Tom Sawyer who?

Tom Sawyer underwear!

Knock, knock...

Who's there?

Diesel.

Diesel who?

Diesel make you feel better!

Knock, knock...

Who's there?

Derek.

Derek who?

Derek get richer and de poor
get poorer!

Knock, knock...

Who's there?

Amish.

Amish who?

Amish you too!

Knock, knock...

Who's there?

Alex.

Alex who?

Alex the questions
round here!

Knock, knock...

Who's there?

Turner.

Turner who?

Turner round, there's a monster
behind you!

Knock, knock...

Who's there?

Adair.

Adair who?

Adair once, but I'm bald now!

Knock, knock...

Who's there?

Snow.

Snow who?

Snow use, I've lost
my key again!

Knock, knock...

Who's there?

Aida.

Aida who?

Aida lot of sweets and now I've got tummy ache!

✳

Knock, knock...

Who's there?

Soup.

Soup who?

Souperman!

✳

Knock, knock...

Who's there?

Sam.

Sam who?

Sam-enchanted evening!

Knock, knock...

Who's there?

Dublin.

Dublin who?

Dublin up with laughter!

Knock, knock...

Who's there?

Toffee.

Toffee who?

Toffee loved is the best feeling
in the world!

Knock, knock...

Who's there?

Yvette.

Yvette who?

Yvette helps lots
of animals.

Knock, knock...

Who's there?

Rhoda.

Rhoda who?

Row, Row, Rhoda boat!

Knock, knock...

Who's there?

Henrietta.

Henrietta who?

Henrietta toadstool, but thought
it was a mushroom!

Knock, knock...

Who's there?

Boo.

Boo who?

Don't get upset, it's only a game!

✳

Knock, knock...

Who's there?

Rita.

Rita who?

Rita book, you might learn something!

Knock, knock...

Who's there?

Kent.

Kent who?

Kent you tell by my voice?

Knock, knock...

Who's there?

Tuna.

Tuna who?

Tuna whole orchestra!

Knock, knock...

Who's there?

Wooden shoe.

Wooden shoe who?

Wooden shoe like to hear
another joke?

Knock, knock...

Who's there?

Sarah.

Sarah who?

Sarah phone I can use?

Knock, knock...

Who's there?

Olive.

Olive who?

Olive right next door to you!

Knock, knock...

Who's there?

Atilla.

Atilla who?

Atilla you open this door
I'm a gonna stand here!

Knock, knock...

Who's there?

Amos.

Amos who?

Amosquito just bit me!

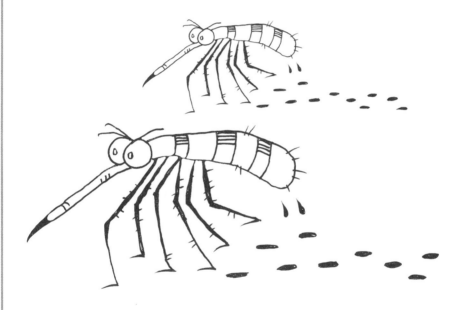

Knock, knock...

Who's there?

Andy.

Andy who?

Andy mosquito bit me again!

Knock, knock...

Who's there?

Eeyore.

Eeyore who?

Eeyore-ways keeps me waiting!

Knock, knock...

Who's there?

Adolf.

Adolf who?

**Adolf ball hit me
in de mouf!**

Knock, knock...

Who's there?

Howl.

Howl who?

**Howl you know unless you open
the door?**

Knock, knock...

Who's there?

Carl.

Carl who?

Carl get you there quicker
than if you walk!

✳

Knock, knock...

Who's there?

Josie.

Josie who?

Josie anyone else out here?

✳

Knock, knock...

Who's there?

Carmen.

Carmen who?

Carmen get it!

Knock, knock...

Who's there?

Jim.

Jim who?

Jim mind if I stay here tonight?

Knock, knock...

Who's there?

Oman.

Oman who?

Oman, you are cute!

Knock, knock...

Who's there?

Cass.

Cass who?

Cass more flies with honey
than vinegar!

Knock, knock...

Who's there?

Amahl.

Amahl who?

Amahl *shook* up!

Knock, knock...

Who's there?

Avenue.

Avenue who?

Avenue guessed yet?

Knock, knock...

Who's there?

Cathy.

Cathy who?

Cathy the doorbell,
it's too dark out here!

Knock, knock...

Who's there?

Barbara.

Barbara who?

Barbara black sheep!

Knock, knock...

Who's there?

I-8.

I-8 who?

I-8 lunch already...
When is dinner?

Knock, knock...

Who's there?

Snow.

Snow who?

Snow use – I can't remember!

Knock, knock...

Who's there?

Little old lady.

Little old lady who?

Your yodelling's getting
much better!

Knock, knock...

Who's there?

McKee.

McKee who?

McKee doesn't fit!

✳

Knock, knock...

Who's there?

Wanda.

Wanda who?

Wanda know how much longer
you're going to keep me hanging
around out here!

SIDE-SPLITTING!

Knock, knock...

Who's there?

Cassie.

Cassie who?

Cassie the wood for the trees!

Knock, knock...

Who's there?

Kent.

Kent who?

Kent you stop asking questions
and open the door!

Knock, knock...

Who's there?

Castor.

Castor who?

Castorblanca!

Knock, knock...

Who's there?

Alma.

Alma who?

Alma time seems to be spent
on this doorstep!

Knock, knock...

Who's there?

Pizza.

Pizza who?

Pizza on Earth and goodwill to all men!

Knock, knock...

Who's there?

Celeste.

Celeste who?

Celeste time I'm going to
tell you this!

Knock, knock...

Who's there?

Pecan.

Pecan who?

Pecan somebody your own size!

Knock, knock...

Who's there?

You are.

You are who?

I'm not Who, I'm me!

Knock, knock...

Who's there?

Phil.

Phil who?

**Phil this cup with sugar please.
I've just run out!**

Knock, knock...

Who's there?

Woody.

Woody who?

**Woody open the door if we
asked him nicely?**

Knock, knock...

Who's there?

Cecil.

Cecil who?

Cecil have music wherever
she goes...!

✳

Knock, knock...

Who's there?

Zone.

Zone who?

Zone shadow scares him!

Knock, knock...

Who's there?

Douglas.

Douglas who?

Douglas is broken!

✳

Knock, knock...

Who's there?

Justin.

Justin who?

Justin time to let me in!

✳

Knock, knock...

Who's there?

Wayne.

Wayne who?

Wayne drops keep falling
on my head!

Knock, knock...

Who's there?

Cash.

Cash who?

I knew you were nuts!

Knock, knock...

Who's there?

Candy.

Candy who?

Candy person who owns this house
please open the door!

Knock, knock...

Who's there?

Matt.

Matt who?

Matt as well settle down, looks like
I'm in for a long wait!

Knock, knock...

Who's there?

Courtney.

Courtney who?

Courtney door, can you open
it and let me loose?

Knock, knock...

Who's there?

Dunce.

Dunce who?

Dunce-ay another word!

Knock, knock...

Who's there?

Aki.

Aki who?

Aki would be really useful right now!

Knock, knock...

Who's there?

Ooze.

Ooze who?

Ooze in charge round here?

Knock, knock...

Who's there?

Señor!

Señor who?

Señor underpants!

Knock, knock...

Who's there?

Donatello.

Donatello who?

Donatello'n me!

Knock, knock...

Who's there

Zeb.

Zeb who?

Zeb better be a good reason for keeping me waiting out here!

Knock, knock...

Who's there?

Ketchup.

Ketchup who?

Ketchup with me and I will tell you.

Knock, knock...
Who's there?
Don Giovanni.
Don Giovanni who?
Don Giovanni talk to me?

Knock, knock...
Who's there?
Ezra.
Ezra who?
Ezra no hope for me?

Knock, knock...
Who's there?
Khan.
Khan who?
Khan you give me a
ride to school?

Knock, knock...

Who's there?

Chas.

Chas who?

Chas pass the key through the
letter box and I'll open the
door myself!

Knock, knock...

Who's there?

Colin.

Colin who?

Colin for a chat!

Knock, knock...

Who's there?

Chad.

Chad who?

Chad to make your
acquaintance!

✳

Knock, knock...

Who's there?

Mary.

Mary who?

Mary Christmas, ho, ho, ho!

Knock, knock...

Who's there?

Cologne.

Cologne who?

Cologne me names won't help!

Knock, knock...

Who's there?

Paula.

Paula who?

Paula up the door handle
and let me in!

Knock, knock...

Who's there?

Morse.

Morse who?

Morse come in as quickly as possible!

Knock, knock...

Who's there?

Cohen.

Cohen who?

Cohen to knock just once more,
then I'm going away!

Knock, knock...

Who's there?

Dwayne.

Dwayne who?

Dwayne in Spain falls mainly
on the plain...!

Knock, knock...

Who's there?

Cher.

Cher who?

Cher and share alike!

Knock, knock...

Who's there?

Farmer.

Farmer who?

Farmer distance
your house looks
much bigger!

Knock, knock...

Who's there?

Cherry.

Cherry who?

Cherry oh, see you later!

Knock, knock...

Who's there?

Bolton...

Bolton who?

Bolton the door!

Knock, knock...

Who's there?

Europe.

Europe who?

Europe'ning the door too slowly,
come on!

Knock, knock...

Who's there?

Barry.

Barry who?

Barry the treasure then no one
will find it!

Knock, knock...

Who's there?

Esther.

Esther who?

Esther anything I can do for you?

Knock, knock...

Who's there?

Osborn.

Osborn who?

Osborn today - it's my birthday!

Knock, knock...

Who's there?

Opera.

Opera who?

Opera-tunity only knocks once,
so make the most of it!

Knock, knock...

Who's there?

Elias.

Elias who?

Elias a terrible thing!

✳

Knock, knock...

Who's there?

Ken.

Ken who?

Ken you come out to play?

✳

Knock, knock...

Who's there?

Alvin.

Alvin who?

**Alvin your heart - just
you vait and see!**

Knock, knock...

Who's there?

Ahmed.

Ahmed who?

Ahmed a big mistake
coming here!

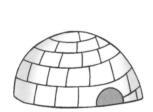

Knock, knock...

Who's there?

Arnie.

Arnie who?

Arnie ever going to let me in?

Knock, knock...

Who's there?

Chuck.

Chuck who?

Chuck and *see* if the door is locked!

Knock, knock...

Who's there?

Ringo.

Ringo who?

Ringo, ringo roses...!

Knock, knock...

Who's there?

Radio.

Radio who?

Radio not,
here I come!

Knock, knock...

Who's there?

Enid.

Enid who?

Enid some more pocket money!

Knock, knock...

Who's there?

Major.

Major who?

Major mind up to open
the door yet?

Knock, knock...

Who's there?

Colleen.

Colleen who?

Colleen up this mess!

Knock, knock...

Who's there?

Enoch.

Enoch who?

Enoch and Enoch,
but no one
answers the door!

Knock, knock...

Who's there?

Isabelle.

Isabelle who?

Isabelle not a good idea?

Knock, knock...

Who's there?

Insurance salesman.

...

... hello...? hello...?

*

Knock, knock...

Who's there?

Cozy.

Cozy who?

Cozy who's knocking!

Knock, knock...

Who's there?

Evan.

Evan who?

Evan and earth!

Knock, knock...

Who's there?

Polly.

Polly who?

**Polly door handle again, I think
it's just stiff!**

Knock, knock...

Who's there?

Colin.

Colin who?

Colin the doctor, I feel ill!

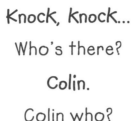

Knock, knock...

Who's there?

Falafel.

Falafel who?

Falafel my *bike* and
cut my knee!

Knock, knock...

Who's there?

Paris.

Paris who?

Paris the thought!

Knock, knock...

Who's there?

Gin.

Gin who?

Gin know how cold it is
out here?

Knock, knock...

Who's there?

Yul.

Yul who?

Yul soon see!

Knock, knock...

Who's there?

Donald.

Donald who?

Donald come baby,
cradle and all!

Knock, knock...

Who's there?

Spock.

Spock who?

Spock the difference between me
and my twin brother!

Knock, knock...

Who's there?

Ella.

Ella who?

Ella-vator. Doesn't that
give you a lift?

Knock, knock...

Who's there?

Mike.

Mike who?

Mike your mind up!

Knock, knock...

Who's there?

Tex.

Tex who?

Tex two to tango.

Knock, knock...

Who's there?

Norm.

Norm who?

Norm more
Mr Nice Guy –
OPEN THIS DOOR!

✸

Knock, knock...

Who's there?

Ferdie.

Ferdie who?

Ferdie last time,
open this door!

✸

Knock, knock...

Who's there?

Mandy.

Mandy who?

Mandy lifeboats!

Knock, knock...

Who's there?

Pasture.

Pasture who?

Pasture bedtime, isn't it?

✳

Knock, knock...

Who's there?

Gandhi.

Gandhi who?

Gandhi cane!

✳

Knock, knock...

Who's there?

Peg.

Peg who?

Peg your pardon,
I've got the wrong door!

Knock, knock...

Who's there?

Candy.

Candy who?

Candy owner of this big red car come and move it off my driveway!

Knock, knock...

Who's there?

Tex.

Tex who?

Tex you ages to open the door!

Knock, knock...

Who's there?

Olivia.

Olivia who?

Olivia, so get out of my house!

Knock, knock...

Who's there?

Batman.

Batman who?

You mean there's more
than one?!

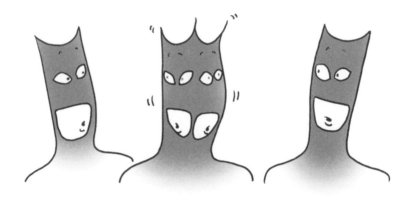

Knock, knock...

Who's there?

Germany.

Germany who?

Germany people knock
on your door?

Knock, knock...

Who's there?

Delhi.

Delhi who?

Delhicatessen!

✳

Knock, knock...

Who's there?

Patrick.

Patrick who?

Patricked me into knocking
on your door!

✳

Knock, knock...

Who's there?

Darren.

Darren who?

Darren young men in their
flying machines!

Knock, knock...

Who's there?

Handel.

Handel who?

Handel with care!

Knock, knock...

Who's there?

Teacher.

Teacher who?

Teacher self for a few days.
I'm having a break!

✳

Knock, knock...

Who's there?

Custer.

Custer who?

Custer lot to find out!

Knock, knock...

Who's there?

Alison.

Alison who?

Alison at the keyhole
sometimes!

✳

Knock, knock...

Who's there?

Mike.

Mike who?

Mike car won't start, can I come
in and use the phone?

Knock, knock...

Who's there?

Abbey.

Abbey who?

**Abbey stung me
on the nose!**

Knock, knock...

Who's there?

Hank.

Hank who?

Hank you!

Knock, knock...

Who's there?

Cy.

Cy who?

Cy'n on the dotted line!

Knock, knock...

Who's there?

Josie.

Josie who?

Josie any reason to keep me
waiting out here?

Knock, knock...

Who's there?

Pat.

Pat who?

Pat yourself on the back!

Knock, knock...

Who's there?

Omelet.

Omelet who?

Omelet smarter
than I look!

Knock, knock...

Who's there?

Zeke.

Zeke who?

Zeke and you will find!

Knock, knock...

Who's there?

Desiree.

Desiree who?

Desiree of sunshine
in my life!

Knock, knock...

Who's there?

Harmon.

Harmon who?

Harmon your side!

Knock, knock...

Who's there?

Harold.

Harold who?

Harold are you?

Knock, knock...

Who's there?

Just Paul.

Just Paul who?

Just Pauling your leg –
it's Steve really!

Knock, knock...

Who's there?

Thumping.

Thumping who?

Thumping green and slimy is
crawling up your back!

Knock, knock...

Who's there?

Daisy.

Daisy who?

Daisy plays, nights he sleeps!

Knock, knock...

Who's there?

Dale.

Dale who?

Dale come if you ask dem!

✳

Knock, knock...

Who's there?

Hugo.

Hugo who?

Hugo your way and I'll go mine!

✳

Knock, knock...

Who's there?

Indy.

Indy who?

Indy hallway is some of my stuff, and
I've come to collect it!

Knock, knock...

Who's there?

Hannah.

Hannah who?

Hannah partridge in a pear tree!

Knock, knock...

Who's there?

Chuck.

Chuck who?

Chuck the key under the door
and I'll let myself in!

Knock, knock...

Who's there?

Darwin.

Darwin who?

I'll be Darwin you
open the door!

Knock, knock...

Who's there?

Bean.

Bean who?

Bean fishing lately?

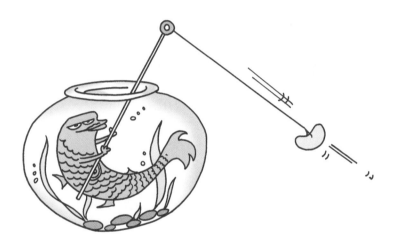

Knock, knock...

Who's there?

Havanna.

Havanna who?

Havanna wonderful time,
wish you were here!

Knock, knock...

Who's there?

Posh.

Posh who?

Posh the door open and you'll see!

Knock, knock...

Who's there?

De Niro.

De Niro who?

De Niro I am to you, the
more I like you!

Knock, knock...

Who's there?

Guess Simon.

Guess Simon who?

Guess Simon the wrong doorstep!

Knock, knock...

Who's there?

Hedda.

Hedda who?

Hedda Nuff! I'm bored of waiting!

Knock, knock...

Who's there?

Eva.

Eva who?

Eva you're deaf or your
doorbell isn't working!

Knock, knock...

Who's there?

Don.

Don who?

Don be afraid...
look into my eyes...
you are feeling sleepy...

✳

Knock, knock...

Who's there?

Yogurt.

Yogurt who?

Yogurt to love my jokes!

✳

Knock, knock...

Who's there?

Harry.

Harry who?

Harry up and answer this door!

Knock, knock...

Who's there?

Cynthia.

Cynthia who?

Cynthia been away
I've missed you!

✳

Knock, knock...

Who's there?

Earl.

Earl who?

Earl be glad to tell you
when you open this door!

✳

Knock, knock...

Who's there?

Curry.

Curry who?

Curry me back home will you?

Knock, knock...

Who's there?

Eddie.

Eddie who?

Eddie body home?

Knock, knock...

Who's there?

Perth.

Perth who?

Perth your lips and whistle!

*

Knock, knock...

Who's there?

Emma.

Emma who?

Emma bit cold out here,
can you let me in?

Knock, knock...

Who's there?

Edith.

Edith who?

Edith, it'll make you feel better!

*

Knock, knock...

Who's there?

Baby.

Baby who?

Baby I shouldn't hab come
round wiv dis cold!

Knock, knock...

Who's there?

Ferrer.

Ferrer who?

Ferrer'vrything there
is a season!

*

Knock, knock...

Who's there?

Dragon.

Dragon who?

Dragon your feet again!

RIB-TICKLING!

Knock, knock...

Who's there?

Datsun.

Datsun who?

Datsun old joke!

Knock, knock...

Who's there?

Yootha.

Yootha who?

Yootha person with the
bicycle for sale?

Knock, knock...

Who's there?

Ella Man.

Ella Man who?

Ella Man-tary, my dear Watson!

Knock, knock...

Who's there?

Emmett.

Emmett who?

Emmett your service!

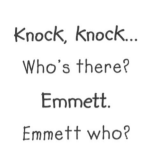

Knock, knock...

Who's there?

Chester.

Chester who?

Chester drawers!

Knock, knock...

Who's there?

Daryl.

Daryl who?

Daryl never be another you!

Knock, knock...

Who's there?

Elsie.

Elsie who?

Elsie you around!

Knock, knock...

Who's there?

Dawn.

Dawn who?

Dawn leave me out here
in the cold!

Knock, knock...

Who's there?

Watson.

Watson who?

Watson TV tonight?

Knock, knock...

Who's there?

Deanna.

Deanna who?

Deanna-mals are restless,
open the cage!

Knock, knock...

Who's there?

Conyers.

Conyers who?

Conyers please open the door!

Knock, knock...

Who's there?

Khan.

Khan who?

Khan down. I only wanted
to say hello!

Knock, knock...

Who's there?

Denise.

Denise who?

Denise are above your ankles!

Knock, knock...

Who's there?

Deena.

Deena who?

Deena hear me the first time?

Knock, knock...

Who's there?

Russell.

Russell who?

Russell up a nice hot cup of tea -
it's freezing out here!

Knock, knock...

Who's there?

Harmony.

Harmony who?

Harmony times do I have to tell you?!
SIGH...

Knock, knock...

Who's there?

Delores.

Delores who?

Delores on the side of the
good guys!

Knock, knock...

Who's there?

Glasgow.

Glasgow who?

Glasgow to the movies!

✳

Knock, knock...

Who's there?

Egbert.

Egbert who?

Egbert no bacon!

✳

Knock, knock...

Who's there?

Diesel.

Diesel who?

Diesel teach me to go around knocking on doors!

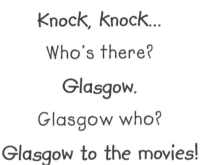

Knock, knock...
Who's there?
Irma.
Irma who?
Irma big girl now!

Knock, knock...
Who's there?
Grant.
Grant who?
Grant you a wish, what is it?

Knock, knock...
Who's there?
Ethan.
Ethan who?
Ethan me out of house and home, you are!

Knock, knock...

Who's there?

Goosey.

Goosey who?

Goosey a doctor,
you don't look well!

Knock, knock...

Who's there?

Amazon.

Amazon who?

Amazon of a gun!

Knock, knock...

Who's there?

Leena.

Leena who?

Leena little closer and
I'll whisper in your ear!

Knock, knock...
Who's there?
Gopher.
Gopher who?
Gopher broke!

Knock, knock...
Who's there?
Lass.
Lass who?
**How long have you
been a cowboy?**

Knock, knock...
Who's there?
Alfred.
Alfred who?
Alfred of the dark!

Knock, knock...

Who's there?

Gable.

Gable who?

Gable to leap buildings in
a single bound!

Knock, knock...

Who's there?

Disguise.

Disguise who?

Disguise the limit!

Knock, knock...

Who's there?

Dinah.

Dinah who?

Dinah shoot until you see the
whites of their eyes!

Knock, knock...

Who's there?

Essen.

Essen who?

Essen it fun to listen to
these jokes?

Knock, knock...

Who's there?

Figs.

Figs who?

Figs the doorbell, it's broken!

Knock, knock...

Who's there?

Denis.

Denis who?

Denis anyone?

Knock, knock...
Who's there?
Gladys.
Gladys who?
Gladys the weekend,
aren't you?

Knock, knock...
Who's there?
Lilian.
Lilian who?
Lilian the garden!

Knock, knock...
Who's there?
Harry.
Harry who?
Harry you been?

Knock, knock...

Who's there?

Diploma.

Diploma who?

Diploma to fix the leak!

Knock, knock...

Who's there?

Florinda.

Florinda who?

Florinda bathroom is wet!

Knock, knock...

Who's there?

Daisy.

Daisy who?

Daisy that you are out, so they steal your stuff!

Knock, knock...

Who's there?

Gordy.

Gordy who?

Gordy-rectly to jail, do not pass Go,
do not collect da money!

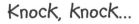

Knock, knock...

Who's there?

Greta.

Greta who?

You Greta on my nerves!

Knock, knock...

Who's there?

Haiti.

Haiti who?

Haiti see a good thing
go to waste!

Knock, knock...

Who's there?

Denver.

Denver who?

Denver the good old days.

Knock, knock...

Who's there?

Desi.

Desi who?

Designated hitter!

✳

Knock, knock...

Who's there?

Gwen.

Gwen who?

Gwen are we going to
get together?

Knock, knock...

Who's there?

Gravy.

Gravy who?

Gravy Crockett!

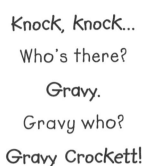

Knock, knock...

Who's there?

Doctor.

Doctor who?

No, Doctor Smith - you sent for me
because you have a cold!

Knock, knock...

Who's there?

Ivor.

Ivor who?

Ivor sore hand from knocking!

Knock, knock...

Who's there?

Juno.

Juno who?

Juno the answer?

Knock, knock...

Who's there?

Pizza.

Pizza who?

Pizza the pie!

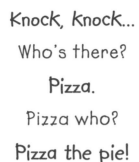

Knock, knock...

Who's there?

Haifa.

Haifa who?

Haifa cake is better than none!

Knock, knock...

Who's there?

Disk.

Disk who?

Disk is a recorded message, please leave your message after the beep!

Knock, knock...

Who's there?

Ammonia.

Ammonia who?

Ammonia little kid!

Knock, knock...

Who's there?

Dana.

Dana who?

Dana talk with your mouth full.

Knock, knock...

Who's there?

Alaska.

Alaska who?

Alaska all my friends to come round
if you don't open up!

Knock, knock...

Who's there?

Hanover.

Hanover who?

Hanover your money!

Knock, knock...

Who's there?

Don.

Don who?

Don Patrol!

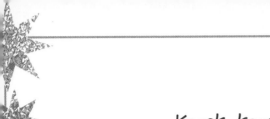

Knock, knock...
Who's there?
Halifax.
Halifax who?
Halifax you if you fax me!

＊

Knock, knock...
Who's there?
Disaster.
Disaster who?
Disaster be my lucky day!

＊

Knock, knock...
Who's there?
Sarah.
Sarah who?
Sarah bell on this door?
I've been knocking for ages!

Knock, knock...

Who's there?

Harriet.

Harriet who?

Harriet up!

✸

Knock, knock...

Who's there?

Dishes.

Dishes who?

Dishes a very bad joke!

✸

Knock, knock...

Who's there?

Giselle.

Giselle who?

Giselle flowers
in there?

Knock, knock...

Who's there?

Mara.

Mara who?

Mara, Mara on the wall!

Knock, knock...

Who's there?

Ahab.

Ahab who?

Ahab to go to the bathroom. Quick, open the door!

Knock, knock...

Who's there?

Fozzie.

Fozzie who?

Fozzie hundredth time, let me in!

Knock, knock...

Who's there?

Freddie.

Freddie who?

Freddie or not here I come!

Knock, knock...

Who's there?

Ivory.

Ivory who?

Ivory strong,
just like Tarzan!

Knock, knock...

Who's there?

Jackson.

Jackson who?

Jackson the telephone,
do you want to talk to him?

Knock, knock...

Who's there?

Dimension.

Dimension who?

Dimension it!

✳

Knock, knock...

Who's there?

Linda.

Linda who?

Linda hand to get this heavy
suitcase up the steps!

Knock, knock...

Who's there?

Freighter.

Freighter who?

I'm Freighter open the door!

Knock, knock...

Who's there?

Ya.

Ya who?

What are you getting so excited about?

Knock, knock...

Who's there?

Wood.

Wood who?

Wood you like to let me in now?

Knock, knock...

Who's there?

Lettuce.

Lettuce who?

Lettuce in and you will find out!

Knock, knock...

Who's there?

Icon.

Icon who?

Icon tell you another knock, knock joke
if you want me to!

Knock, knock...

Who's there?

Dot.

Dot who?

Dots for me to know, and you
to find out.

Knock, knock...

Who's there?

Karl.

Karl who?

I'll Karl again another day
when you're feeling better!

Knock, knock...

Who's there?

Toby.

Toby who?

Toby or not to be!

Knock, knock...

Who's there?

Cargo.

Cargo who?

Cargo beep! beep!

Knock, knock...

Who's there?

Island.

Island who?

Island on your
roof with my
parachute!

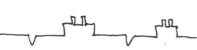

Knock, knock...

Who's there?

Winnie Thup.

Winnie Thup who?

And Tigger came too!

Knock, knock...

Who's there?

Nobel.

Nobel who?

Nobel, that's why I knocked!

✳

Knock, knock...

Who's there?

Ben.

Ben who?

Ben wondering what you're up to!

✳

Knock, knock...

Who's there?

Butcher.

Butcher who?

Butcher didn't know it was me
at the door, did you?

Knock, knock...

Who's there?

Wendy.

Wendy who?

Wendy wind blows de cradle
will rock.

Knock, knock...

Who's there?

Ford.

Ford who?

Ford he's a jolly good fellow!

Knock, knock...

Who's there?

Jaws.

Jaws who?

Jaws truly!

Knock, knock...

Who's there?

Rabbit.

Rabbit who?

**Rabbit up carefully,
it's a present!**

Knock, knock...

Who's there?

Thayer.

Thayer who?

**Thayer thorry or I'll throw thith
pie in your face!**

Knock, knock...

Who's there?

Fonda.

Fonda who?

Fonda you!

Knock, knock...

Who's there?

Butternut.

Butternut who?

Butternut squash the eggs!

✳

Knock, knock...

Who's there?

Hans.

Hans who?

Hans off the table!

✳

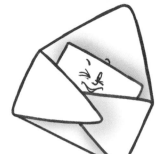

Knock, knock...

Who's there?

Red.

Red who?

Red your letters,
you can have them
back now!

Knock, knock...

Who's there?

Dexter.

Dexter who?

Dexter halls with
boughs of holly.

Knock, knock...

Who's there?

Aretha.

Aretha who?

Aretha holly on your door.

Knock, knock...

Who's there?

A little girl.

A little girl who?

A little girl who can't reach the
doorbell!

Knock, knock...

Who's there?

Sacha.

Sacha who?

Sacha fuss over nothing!

✳

Knock, knock...

Who's there?

Banana.

Banana who?

Knock, knock...

Who's there?

Banana.

Banana who?

Knock, knock...

Who's there?

Orange.

Orange who?

Orange you glad I didn't
say banana?

Knock, knock...

Who's there?

Dwayne.

Dwayne who?

Dwayne the bathtub,
it's overflowing!

Knock, knock...

Who's there?

Aaron.

Aaron who?

Aaron the side of caution!

Knock, knock...

Who's there?

Heidi.

Heidi who?

Heidi-clare war on you!

✷

Knock, knock...

Who's there?

Scold.

Scold who?

Scold outside.

Knock, knock...

Who's there?

Kline.

Kline who?

Kline of you to invite me round!

Knock, knock...

Who's there?

Water.

Water who?

Water you doing in my house?

Knock, knock...

Who's there?

Wendy.

Wendy who?

Wendy you want me to
call round again?

Knock, knock...

Who's there?

Lisbon.

Lisbon who?

Lisbon to see me, now she's
come to see you!

Knock, knock...

Who's there?

Sid.

Sid who?

Sid you'd be ready by three –
where are you?!

Knock, knock...

Who's there?

Beethoven.

Beethoven who?

Beethoven is too hot!

Knock, knock...

Who's there?

Pearce.

Pearce who?

Pearce this balloon with a pin!

Knock, knock...

Who's there?

Sally.

Sally who?

**Sally-brate the best moments
of your life!**

Knock, knock...

Who's there?

Deduct.

Deduct who?

Donald Deduct!

✳

Knock, knock...

Who's there?

Dill.

Dill who?

Dill we meet again!

✳

Knock, knock...

Who's there?

Paul.

Paul who?

Paul the other one,
it's got bells on!

Knock, knock...

Who's there?

Felix.

Felix who?

Felix my ice cream,
I'll lick his!

Knock, knock...

Who's there?

Luke.

Luke who?

Luke through the keyhole
and you'll see!

Knock, knock...

Who's there?

Carla.

Carla who?

Carla taxi, I'm leaving!

Knock, knock...

Who's there?

Violet.

Violet who?

Violet the cat out of the bag!

Knock, knock...

Who's there?

Butter.

Butter who?

Butter let me in!

Knock, knock...

Who's there?

Theodore.

Theodore who?

Theodore is stuck and
it won't open!

Knock, knock...

Who's there?

Giraffe.

Giraffe who?

**Giraffe to ask me that
stupid question?**

Knock, knock...

Who's there?

Larva.

Larva who?

Larva cup of coffee.

Knock, knock...

Who's there?

Jools.

Jools who?

Jools like these should be worth a lot of money!

✳

Knock, knock...

Who's there?

Ivan.

Ivan who?

Ivan infectious disease, so watch out!

✳

Knock, knock...

Who's there?

Ethan.

Ethan who?

Ethan too much makes you fat!

Knock, knock...

Who's there?

Fresno.

Fresno who?

Rudolf the Fresno reindeer!

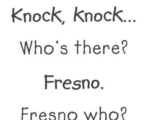

Knock, knock...

Who's there?

Jez.

Jez who?

Jez me, that's who!

Knock, knock...

Who's there?

Chris.

Chris who?

Christmas is coming and the
goose is getting fat!

Knock, knock...

Who's there?

Genoa.

Genoa who?

Genoa any new jokes?

✳

Knock, knock...

Who's there?

Henrietta.

Henrietta who?

Henrietta worm that was
in his apple!

KNEE-SLAPPING!

Knock, knock...

Who's there?

Morgan.

Morgan who?

Morgan you could ever imagine!

＊

Knock, knock...

Who's there?

Tessa.

Tessa who?

Tessa long time for you
to open the door!

＊

Knock, knock...

Who's there?

Hardy.

Hardy who?

Hardy har, fooled you!

Knock, knock...

Who's there?

Teresa.

Teresa who?

Teresa jolly good fellow!

Knock, knock...

Who's there?

Whoo ooo oooo ooo...

Whoo ooo oooo ooo who?

Ah, this must be the haunted house!

Knock, knock...

Who's there?

Congo.

Congo who?

Congo out, I'm grounded!

Knock, knock...

Who's there?

Wendy.

Wendy who?

Wendy red, red robin comes bob,
bob bobbin' along, along!

Knock, knock...

Who's there?

Courtney.

Courtney who?

Courtney good soccer
matches lately?

Knock, knock...

Who's there?

Ray.

Ray who?

Ray-ders of the Lost Ark!

✳

Knock, knock...

Who's there?

Chris.

Chris who?

Chris P. Bacon,
in time for breakfast!

Knock, knock...
Who's there?
Jess.
Jess who?
Jess me and my
shadow!

Knock, knock...
Who's there?
May.
May who?
May I come in?

Knock, knock...
Who's there?
Jethro.
Jethro who?
Jethro this at me?

Knock, knock...

Who's there?

Callista.

Callista who?

Callista warm reception?

Knock, knock...

Who's there?

Seymour.

Seymour who?

Seymour of me by opening
the door!

Knock, knock...

Who's there?

Sid.

Sid who?

Sid down and I'll explain!

Knock, knock...

Who's there?

Usher.

Usher who?

Usher wish you would let me in!

Knock, knock...

Who's there?

Vince.

Vince who?

Vince some time since
I saw you last!

Knock, knock...

Who's there?

Icing.

Icing who?

Icing carols - you give
me money!

Knock, knock...

Who's there?

Plato.

Plato who?

Plato fish with lots of ketchup, please!

Knock, knock...

Who's there?

Alligator.

Alligator who?

Alligator sandwiches early,
so she sent me to get
some more!

Knock, knock...

Who's there?

Parson.

Parson who?

Parson through and I thought
I'd say hello!

Knock, knock...

Who's there?

Belle.

Belle who?

Belle doesn't work, so I'm
having to knock!

Knock, knock...

Who's there?

Jaffa.

Jaffa who?

Jaffa keep me waiting?

✳

Knock, knock...

Who's there?

Walter.

Walter who?

Walter strange thing to ask!

✳

Knock, knock...

Who's there?

Amanda.

Amanda who?

**Amanda fix
the boiler!**

Knock, knock...

Who's there?

Jerome.

Jerome who?

Jerome at last!

Knock, knock...

Who's there?

Will.

Will who?

**Will wait out here until
you let us in!**

Knock, knock...

Who's there?

Norbut.

Norbut who?

Norbut a kid!

Knock, knock...

Who's there?

CD.

CD who?

CDs fingers?
They're freezing – let me in!

✳

Knock, knock...

Who's there?

You.

You who?

You-who to you, too!

Knock, knock...

Who's there?

Fitz.

Fitz who?

Fitz not too much trouble, can
you please open the door?

Knock, knock...

Who's there?

Olly.

Olly who?

Olly need is love!

Knock, knock...

Who's there?

Teddy.

Teddy who?

Teddy is the beginning of the
rest of your life!

Knock, knock...

Who's there?

Otto.

Otto who?

Ottold you two seconds ago!

Knock, knock...

Who's there?

Ozzie.

Ozzie who?

Ozzie you still have the same front door you did the last time I called!

Knock, knock...

Who's there?

Lucinda.

Lucinda who?

Lucinda sky with diamonds!

Knock, knock...

Who's there?

Brewster.

Brewster who?

Brewster wakes me up
every morning singing
cock-a-doodle-do!

✳

Knock, knock...

Who's there?

Misty.

Misty who?

Misty door bell again!

✳

Knock, knock...

Who's there?

Olive.

Olive who?

Olive none of your lip!

Knock, knock...

Who's there?

Bart.

Bart who?

Bart time you opened this door!

Knock, knock...

Who's there?

Paul.

Paul who?

Paul up a chair and
I'll tell you!

Knock, knock...

Who's there?

Ivan.

Ivan who?

Ivan idea you will
know as soon as you
open the door!

Knock, knock...

Who's there?

Ida.

Ida who?

Ida know why I love you like I do!

Knock, knock...

Who's there?

Lester.

Lester who?

Lester worry about!

Knock, knock...

Who's there?

Police.

Police who?

Police open the door and
find out!

Knock, knock...

Who's there?

Willy.

Willy who?

Willy hurry up and let me in!

Knock, knock...

Who's there?

Fred.

Fred who?

Fred you'll have to let me in!

Knock, knock...

Who's there?

Mustapha.

Mustapha who?

Mustapha good reason to
keep me waiting!

Knock, knock...

Who's there?

Jester.

Jester who?

Jester day, you were out.

Today, you're in!

Knock, knock...

Who's there?

Constance.

Constance who?

Constance snoring is keeping me awake!

Knock, knock...

Who's there?

Mickey.

Mickey who?

Mickey fell down the drain,
can you help me find it?

Knock, knock...

Who's there?

Interrupting cow.

Interrupt... MOOOOO!

Knock, knock...

Who's there?

Butcher.

Butcher who?

Butcher said I could come
and visit you!

Knock, knock...

Who's there?

Joanna.

Joanna who?

Joanna have a guess?

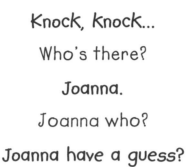

Knock, knock...

Who's there?

Mouse.

Mouse who?

Mouse get a key of my own!

Knock, knock...

Who's there?

Arthur.

Arthur who?

Arthur minute and I'll show
you my identification!

✳

Knock, knock...

Who's there?

Lefty.

Lefty who?

Lefty home on your own again!

✳

Knock, knock...

Who's there?

Dan.

Dan who?

Dan just stand there -
let me in!

Knock, knock...

Who's there?

Wendy.

Wendy who?

Wendy come to collect the rent,
I'm off!

Knock, knock...

Who's there?

Shirley.

Shirley who?

Shirley you know the sound
of my voice by now!

Knock, knock...

Who's there?

Goat.

Goat who?

Goat to the door and find out!

Knock, knock...

Who's there?

Aware.

Aware who?

Aware, aware has my
little dog gone?

Knock, knock...

Who's there?

A ghost.

A ghost who?

Thought it would
scare you!

Knock, knock...

Who's there?

I love.

I love who?

I don't know, you tell me!

Knock, knock...

Who's there?

Honor Claire.

Honor Claire who?

Honor Claire day, you can
see forever!

Knock, knock...

Who's there?

Aardvark.

Aardvark who?

Aardvark a million miles for
one of your smiles!

Knock, knock...

Who's there?

Wallace.

Wallace who?

Wallace a fine mess you got me into!

✳

Knock, knock...

Who's there?

Elvis.

Elvis who?

Elvis is a complete
waste of time, I'm off!

✳

Knock, knock...

Who's there?

Howard.

Howard who?

Howard you know if you won't
even open the door?

Knock, knock...

Who's there?

Our Tell.

Our Tell who?

Our Tell you what I want,
what I really really want!

Knock, knock...

Who's there?

Homer.

Homer who?

Homer goodness! I can't
remember my name!

Knock, knock...

Who's there?

Oliver.

Oliver who?

Oliver across the road from you!

Knock, knock...

Who's there?

Boo.

Boo who?

Bootiful front door you have.

Knock, knock...

Who's there?

Fletch.

Fletch who?

Fletch a bucket of water, your
house is on fire!

Knock, knock...
Who's there?
Tank.
Tank who?
You're welcome!

Knock, knock...
Who's there?
Arnold.
Arnold who?
Arnold friend
you haven't seen
for years!

Knock, knock...
Who's there?
Fergie.
Fergie who?
Fergiedness sake, let me in!

Will you remember me tomorrow?

Of course!

Will you remember me in a year?

Certainly.

Will you remember me in five years?

For sure!

Will you remember me
in ten years?

Yes!

Knock, knock...

Who's there?

You see, you've forgotten
me already!

Knock, knock...

Who's there?

Igloo.

Igloo who?

Igloo knew Suzie like
I know Suzie!

Knock, knock...

Who's there?

Norma Lee.

Norma Lee who?

Norma Lee I don't go around knocking
on doors, but do you want to buy a
set of encyclopedias?

Knock, knock...

Who's there?

Dime.

Dime who?

Dime to tell another knock, knock joke!

Knock, knock...

Who's there?

Despair.

Despair who?

Despair room is full of junk!

Knock, knock...

Who's there?

Accordion.

Accordion who?

Accordion to the weather forecast,
it's going to rain tomorrow!

Knock, knock...

Who's there?

Ben.

Ben who?

Ben down and tie
your shoelaces!

Knock, knock...

Who's there?

Yah.

Yah who?

Yahoo! Ride'em, cowboy!

Knock, knock...

Who's there?

Handsome.

Handsome who?

Handsome money
through the keyhole
and I'll tell you more!

Knock, knock...

Who's there?

Telly.

Telly who?

Telly your friend to come out!

Knock, knock...

Who's there?

Closure.

Closure who?

Closure mouth when you're eating!

Knock, knock...

Who's there?

Argue.

Argue who?

Argue going to let me in or not???

Knock, knock...

Who's there?

Howard.

Howard who?

Howard is it to recognize my voice?
I'm your best friend!

Knock, knock...

Who's there?

Buddha.

Buddha who?

Buddha this slice of
bread for me!

Knock, knock...

Who's there?

Julia.

Julia who?

Julia want some milk and cookies?

Knock, knock...

Who's there?

Kay.

Kay who?

Kay, L, M, N, O, P, Q, R, S, T, U,
V, W, X, Y, Z!

Knock, knock...

Who's there?

Yachts.

Yachts who?

Yachts up, doc?!?

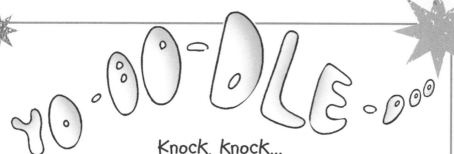

Knock, knock...

Who's there?

Yodel.

Yodel who?

Yodel who to you too! Let's form
a yodelling duo!

*

Knock, knock...

Who's there?

Havelock.

Havelock who?

Havelock put on your door!

*

Knock, knock...

Who's there?

Scott.

Scott who?

Scott nothing to do with you!

Knock, knock...

Who's there?

U-8.

U-8 who?

U-8 my lunch!

✳

Knock, knock...

Who's there?

Amanda.

Amanda who?

Amanda the table!

Knock, knock...

Who's there?

Hammond.

Hammond who?

Hammond eggs for breakfast.

✳

Knock, knock...

Who's there?

Eyesore.

Eyesore who?

Eyesore do like you!

✳

Knock, knock...

Who's there?

C-2.

C-2 who?

C-2 it that you don't forget my
name next time!

Knock, knock...

Who's there?

Costas.

Costas who?

Costas a fortune to get here!

Knock, knock...

Who's there?

Ike.

Ike who?

Ike can't stop laughing!

Knock, knock...

Who's there?

Element.

Element who?

Element to tell you that she can't see you today!

Knock, knock...

Who's there?

Olive.

Olive who?

Olive you!

Knock, knock...

Who's there?

Lionel.

Lionel who?

Lionel bite you if you put your
head in its mouth!!!

Knock, knock...
Who's there?
Lauren.
Lauren who?
Lauren order!

Knock, knock...
Who's there?
Cereal.
Cereal who?
Cereal pleasure to meet you!

Knock, knock...

Who's there?

Cam.

Cam who?

Camelot is where King Arthur lived!

Knock, knock...

Who's there?

Max.

Max who?

Max no difference!

Knock, knock...

Who's there?

Eamonn.

Eamonn who?

Eamonn a good mood today,
can I come in?

Knock, knock...

Who's there?

Eileen.

Eileen who?

Eileen down to tie my shoe!

Knock, knock...

Who's there?

Mae.

Mae who?

Mae be I'll tell you or
maybe I won't!

Knock, knock...

Who's there?

Haden.

Haden who?

Haden seek!

Knock, knock...

Who's there?

Willy.

Willy who?

**Willy lend me a street map?
I'm a stranger in town!**

✳

Knock, knock...

Who's there?

Zany.

Zany who?

Zany body home?

Knock, knock...

Who's there?

Dad.

Dad who?

Dad fuel to the fire!

Knock, knock...

Who's there?

Hawaii.

Hawaii who?

I'm fine, Hawaii you?

Knock, knock...

Who's there?

Postman Pat.

Have you got a parcel?

No, but I've got a
black and white cat!

Knock, knock...

Who's there?

Candace.

Candace who?

Candace be true?

Knock, knock...

Who's there?

Ear.

Ear who?

Ear you are!
I've been looking for you!

Knock, knock...

Who's there?

May.

May who?

May the force be with you!

Knock, knock...

Who's there?

Queen.

Queen who?

Queen as a whistle!

Knock, knock...

Who's there?

Waiter.

Waiter who?

**Waiter minute, this isn't
my house!**

Knock, knock...

Who's there?

Amory.

Amory who?

Amory Christmas!

Knock, knock...

Who's there?

Waddle.

Waddle who?

Waddle you give me if
I promise to go away?

Knock, knock...

Who's there?

The Vampire.

The Vampire who?

The Vampire State Building!

✳

Knock, knock...

Who's there?

Rufus.

Rufus who?

Rufus on fire!

HIGH-FIVING!

Knock, knock...

Who's there?

Leaf.

Leaf who?

Leaf me alone!

✻

Knock, knock...

Who's there?

Abbott.

Abbott who?

Abbott time you opened
this door!

✻

Knock, knock...

Who's there?

Juicy.

Juicy who?

Juicy what I just saw?

Knock, knock...

Who's there?

Eye.

Eye who?

Eye know who you are!

Knock, knock...

Who's there?

Who.

Who who?

Is there an owl
in there?

Knock, knock...

Who's there?

Farrah.

Farrah who?

Farrah'nough!

Knock, knock...

Who's there?

Zizi.

Zizi who?

Zizi when you know how!

Knock, knock...

Who's there?

Bach.

Bach who?

Bach to work, you slackers!

Knock, knock...

Who's there?

Mabel.

Mabel who?

Mabel doesn't
ring either!

Knock, knock...

Who's there?

Les.

Les who?

Les go for a swim!

Knock, knock...

Who's there?

Ivan.

Ivan who?

Ivan enormous snake
in my pouch!

Knock, knock...

Who's there?

Cattle.

Cattle who?

Cattle purr if you stroke it!

Knock, knock...

Who's there?

Nadia.

Nadia who?

Just Nadia head if you understand
what I'm saying!

Knock, knock...

Who's there?

I don't know.

I don't know who?

I told you I don't know.
Why don't you believe me?

✳

Knock, knock...

Who's there?

Annie.

Annie who?

Annie body calls, I'm out!

✳

Knock, knock...

Who's there?

Zookeeper.

Zookeeper who?

Zookeeper away from him!

Knock, knock...
Who's there?
Fangs.
Fangs who?
Fangs for the memory!

✳

Knock, knock...
Who's there?
Lionel.
Lionel who?
Lionel get you nowhere, better
tell the truth!

✳

Knock, knock...
Who's there?
Lisa.
Lisa who?
Lisa you can do is letta me in!

Knock, knock...

Who's there?

Madrid.

Madrid who?

Madrid you wash my jeans?

Knock, knock...

Who's there?

Anita.

Anita who?

Anita borrow
a pencil!

Knock, knock...

Who's there?

Spell.

Spell who?

W...H...O!

Knock, knock...

Who's there?

Blue.

Blue who?

Blue away with the wind!

Knock, knock...

Who's there?

Venice.

Venice who?

Venice this door going
to open?

Knock, knock...

Who's there?

Bella.

Bella who?

Bella bottom
trousers!

Knock, knock...

Who's there?

Imogen.

Imogen who?

Imogen life without chocolate!

Knock, knock...

Who's there?

Nuisance.

Nuisance who?

What's nuisance yesterday?

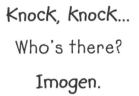

Knock, knock...

Who's there?

Vassar.

Vassar who?

Vassar girl like you doing in a place like this?

Knock, knock...

Who's there?

Ike.

Ike who?

Ike could have danced all night!

Knock, knock...

Who's there?

Thaddeus.

Thaddeus who?

To be or not to be, Thaddeus
the question!

Knock, knock...

Who's there?

Jack.

Jack who?

Jackpot! We've won first prize!

Knock, knock...

Who's there?

Edwin.

Edwin who?

Edwin a cup if he could
run faster!

Knock, knock...

Who's there?

Bargain.

Bargain who?

Bargain up the wrong tree!

Knock, knock...

Who's there?

Luck.

Luck who?

Luck through the key hole
and you'll find out!

Knock, knock...

Who's there?

Tara.

Tara who?

Tara-ra boom-de-ay!

Knock, knock...

Who's there?

Gorilla.

Gorilla who?

Gorilla cheese sandwich for me
and I'll be right over!

Knock, knock...

Who's there?

Howie.

Howie who?

I'm fine, how are you!

Knock, knock...

Who's there?

Abyssinia.

Abyssinia who?

Abyssinia behind bars one
of these days!

Knock, knock...

Who's there?

Yubin.

Yubin who?

Yubin eating garlic
again?

Knock, knock...

Who's there?

Lenny.

Lenny who?

Lenny in, I'm hungry!

Knock, knock...

Who's there?

Sherwood.

Sherwood who?

Sherwood like to meet you!

Knock, knock...

Who's there?

Carol.

Carol who?

Carol down the hill,
call the police!

Knock, knock...

Who's there?

Honey bee.

Honey bee who?

Honey bee a sweetie
and let me in!

Knock, knock...

Who's there?

Ears.

Ears who?

Ears looking at you!

Knock, knock...

Who's there?

Theodore.

Theodore who?

Theodore wasn't open
so I knocked!

Knock, knock...

Who's there?

Boliva.

Boliva who?

Boliva me, I know what
I'm talking about!

Knock, knock!

Who's there?

Vidor.

Vidor who?

Vidor better open soon!

Knock, knock...

Who's there?

Sam.

Sam who?

Sam person who knocked on
the door last time!

Knock, knock...

Who's there?

Trixie.

Trixie who?

Trixie couldn't do because
he was a bad magician!

Knock, knock...

Who's there?

Albee.

Albee who?

Albee a monkey's uncle!

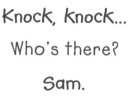

Knock, knock...

Who's there?

Thermos.

Thermos who?

Thermos be a better
knock, knock joke than this!

Knock, knock...

Who's there?

Hand.

Hand who?

Hand over your wallet, this is a raid!

Knock, knock...

Who's there?

Bjorn.

Bjorn who?

Bjorn with a silver spoon
in his mouth!

Knock, knock...

Who's there?

Adelia.

Adelia who?

Adelia the cards and we'll play a game!

Knock, knock...

Who's there?

Arf.

Arf who?

Arf full or
arf empty!

Knock, knock...

Who's there?

Ina.

Ina who?

Ina minute I'm going to knock
this door down!

Knock, knock...

Who's there?

Eugenie.

Eugenie who?

Eugenie from the bottle who will grant you three wishes.

Knock, knock...

Who's there?

Ada.

Ada who?

Ada burger for lunch!

Knock, knock...

Who's there?

Veal chop.

Veal chop who?

Veal chop around and *see* vot
bargains vee can pick up!

Knock, knock...

Who's there?

Chile.

Chile who?

Chile out tonight, isn't it!

Knock, knock...

Who's there?

Formosa.

Formosa who?

Formosa the summer I was
away on vacation!

Knock, knock...

Who's there?

Zippy.

Zippy who?

Zippy dee-doo-dah, zippy dee-ay!

Knock, knock...

Who's there?

Butter.

Butter who?

Butter open quick,
I have to go to the bathroom!

Knock, knock...

Who's there?

Arthur.

Arthur who?

Arthur any more cookies
in the jar?

Knock, knock...

Who's there?

Truffle.

Truffle who?

Truffle with you is that you are so shy!

Knock, knock...

Who's there?

Witches.

Witches who?

Witches the way to go home?

Knock, knock...

Who's there?

Reed.

Reed who?

Reed-turn to sender,
address unknown!

Knock, knock...

Who's there?

Lucretia.

Lucretia who?

Lucretia from the Black Lagoon!

Knock, knock...

Who's there?

Archie.

Archie who?

Bless you!

Knock, knock...

Who's there?

Jeannette.

Jeannette who?

Jeanette has holes in it,
the fish will escape!

✳

Knock, knock...

Who's there?

Anthem.

Anthem who?

Anthem prince seeking pretty princess.

✳

Knock, knock...

Who's there?

Apple.

Apple who?

Apple your hair if you
don't let me in!

Knock, knock...

Who's there?

Arbus.

Arbus who?

Arbus leaves in 5 minutes!

Knock, knock...

Who's there?

Ollie.

Ollie who?

Ollie time you say that,
I wish you would cut it out!

Knock, knock...

Who's there?

Anna.

Anna who?

Anna gonna tell you!

Knock, knock...

Who's there?

Galway.

Galway who?

Galway, you're annoying me!

Knock, knock...

Who's there?

Anne Boleyn.

Anne Boleyn who?

Anne Boleyn alley!

Knock, knock...

Who's there?

Annetta.

Annetta who?

Annetta wisecrack and you're
out of here!

Knock, knock...

Who's there?

Cole.

Cole who?

Cole as a
cucumber!

Knock, knock...

Who's there?

Bjorn.

Bjorn who?

Bjorn to be wild!

Knock, knock...

Who's there?

Don Juan.

Don Juan who?

Don Juan to go to school today?

*

Knock, knock...

Who's there?

Lion.

Lion who?

Lion down on the job again!

*

Knock, knock...

Who's there?

Anita.

Anita who?

Anita you like I need a hole
in the head!

Knock, knock...

Who's there?

Alpaca.

Alpaca who?

**Alpaca the trunk, you packa
the suitcase!**

Knock, knock...

Who's there?

Izzy.

Izzy who?

Izzy come, Izzy go!

Knock, knock...

Who's there?

Omar.

Omar who?

**Omar goodness gracious,
wrong door!**

Knock, knock...

Who's there?

Moo.

Moo who?

Well, make up your mind,
are you a cow or an owl?

Knock, knock...

Who's there?

Oink moo.

Oink moo who?

You are confused, aren't you?!

Knock, knock...

Who's there?

Haydn.

Haydn who?

Haydn in this cupboard
is boring!

✳

Knock, knock...

Who's there?

Andrew.

Andrew who?

Andrew a picture!

✳

Knock, knock...

Who's there?

Amy.

Amy who?

Amy fraid I've forgotten!

Knock, knock...

Who's there?

Ginger.

Ginger who?

Ginger hear the doorbell?

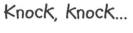

Knock, knock...

Who's there?

Phyllis.

Phyllis who?

Phyllis bucket of water,
please!

Knock, knock...

Who's there?

Beezer.

Beezer who?

Beezer black and yellow and
make honey!

Knock, knock...

Who's there?

Jess.

Jess who?

I give up, who?

✳

Knock, knock...

Who's there?

Ben.

Ben who?

Ben knocking on this door
all morning!

✳

Knock, knock...

Who's there?

Althea.

Althea who?

Althea later, alligator!

Knock, knock...

Who's there?

Allied.

Allied who?

Allied, so sue me!

※

Knock, knock...

Who's there?

Diana.

Diana who?

Diana of thirst.
Can I have a glass
of water please?

※

Knock, knock...

Who's there?

Alfie.

Alfie who?

Alfie terrible if you leave!

Knock, knock...

Who's there?

Alva.

Alva who?

Alva heart!

✳

Knock, knock...

Who's there?

Cow-go.

Cow-go who?

No, cow go MOO!!!

Knock, knock...
Who's there?
Belize.
Belize who?
Belize in yourself!

✸

Knock, knock...
Who's there?
Alaska.
Alaska who?
Alaska again, please
open the door!

✸

Knock, knock...
Who's there?
Brigham.
Brigham who?
Brigham back my sunshine
to me!

Knock, knock...

Who's there?

Aunt Lou.

Aunt Lou who?

Aunt Lou do you think you are?

Knock, knock...

Who's there?

Alfalfa.

Alfalfa who?

Alfalfa you, if you give
me a kiss!

★

Knock, knock...

Who's there?

Berlin.

Berlin who?

Berlin the water for my
hard-boiled eggs!

Knock, knock...

Who's there?

Bernadette.

Bernadette who?

**Bernadette all my dinner
and now I'm starving!**

Knock, knock...

Who's there?

Ivor.

Ivor who?

**Ivor good mind not
to tell you now!**

Knock, knock...

Who's there?

Harry.

Harry who?

Harry up! There's a monster
behind us!

Knock, knock...

Who's there?

Turkey.

Turkey who?

Turkey and find out!

Knock, knock...

Who's there?

Champ.

Champ who?

Champ-oo in my eyes. I can't see!

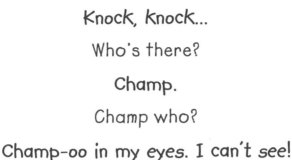

Knock, knock...

Who's there?

Eugene.

Eugene who?

Eugene, me Tarzan!

Knock, knock...

Who's there?

Topic.

Topic who?

Topic a wild flower is
against the law!

Knock, knock...

Who's there?

Steve.

Steve who?

Steve upper lip!

Knock, knock...

Who's there?

Axl.

Axl who?

Axl me nicely and I might
just tell you!

Knock, Knock...

Who's there?

Shelby.

Shelby who?

Shelby coming round the mountain
when she comes!

Knock, knock...

Who's there?

Chicken.

Chicken who?

Chicken the oven, I can smell burning!

Knock, knock...

Who's there?

Cheese.

Cheese who?

Cheese a cute girl!

Knock, knock...

Who's there?

Wade.

Wade who?

Wade down upon the Swanee River!

✳

Knock, knock...

Who's there?

Ice cream.

Ice cream who?

Ice cream every time I see a ghost!

✳

Knock, knock...

Who's there?

Mary Lee.

Mary Lee who?

Mary Lee, Mary Lee, life is but a dream! Row, row...

Knock, knock...

Who's there?

Isadore.

Isadore who?

Isadore on the right way round?

✸

Knock, knock...

Who's there?

Patty O.

Patty O who?

Patty O furniture!

✸

Knock, knock...

Who's there?

Iona.

Iona who?

Iona have eyes
for you!

Knock, knock...

Who's there?

Carol.

Carol who?

**Carol go if you switch
the ignition on!**

Knock, knock...

Who's there?

Dakota.

Dakota who?

Dakota is too small!

Knock, knock...

Who's there?

Abba, Abba.

Abba, Abba Who?

**Abba Merry Christmas and
Abba Happy New Year!**

Knock, knock...

Who's there?

Gopher.

Gopher who?

Gopher help, I'm stuck in the mud!

✳

Knock, knock...

Who's there?

Scott.

Scott who?

Scott a creepy look about it, this place. I think it's haunted!

Knock, knock...

Who's there?

Esau.

Esau who?

Esau you in the bath!

Knock, knock...

Who's there?

Hippo.

Hippo who?

Hippo-hop, dance till I drop!

Knock, knock...

Who's there?

Brad.

Brad who?

Brad news, I'm afraid – this is
the last knock, knock joke!